DANCE OF FREEDOM

This title is part of a series of books entitled
ESSENTIAL INDIA EDITIONS. Each book in the series will explore a
foundational aspect of the country in new and thought-provoking ways.
~

ALSO IN THIS SERIES

Our Living Constitution: A Concise Introduction & Commentary
by Shashi Tharoor

Song of India: A Study of the National Anthem
by Rudrangshu Mukherjee

Language of the Immortals: A Concise Study of Sanskrit
by G. N. Devy

The Mysterious Life of Tigers: A Book of Discovery
by Valmik Thapar

DANCE
OF
FREEDOM

A Short History of Bharata Natyam

LEELA SAMSON

ALEPH

ALEPH

ALEPH BOOK COMPANY
An independent publishing firm
promoted by *Rupa Publications India*

First published in India in 2025
by Aleph Book Company
161-B/4, Gulmohar House,
Yusuf Sarai Community Centre,
New Delhi 110049

ISBN: 978-93-6523-367-4

1 3 5 7 9 10 8 6 4 2

Pushpanjali

To Rukmini Devi Arundale—my mentor.

∾

'If you have knowledge,
let others light their candles in it.'
—Margaret Fuller

∿

CONTENTS

PROLOGUE

*A*rangetram was not a word that I was familiar with as a child. Even when studying Bharata Natyam at Kalakshetra—the apex dance academy situated in Madras—no one talked about it. By the time I finished the Madras Matriculation, I had an inkling of what it was, but had no reason to want to do it. This was because Rukmini Devi, the founder of the academy, did not wish for us to learn the dance with that intent in mind. It was not a goal to aspire for.

My parents knew little about the dance. They therefore erred on the side of wanting to do what was right by me. Their South Indian friends in Bombay, perhaps the Swaminathans whose only daughter also studied at Kalakshetra, advised them to ask Rukmini Devi if I should do my arangetram. I am not sure what exactly transpired. This I do know that neither I, nor any of my classmates had any thoughts about it. But it was arranged by my father to be held in

Bombay at the start of the summer holidays of 1970. I would prepare for it with my teachers in Madras. The musicians would come to Bombay, where it would be held on 7 May, a day after my nineteenth birthday.

My father made meticulous arrangements. I reached Bombay a couple of days earlier to be able to spend time with my grandmother and family. The musicians were to arrive on 6 May. On the 5th, I heard whispers about the musicians having missed their train! Someone had slipped up and it was not my father. They reached the station on time, but a whole day late! Fortunately, they alighted the same train but would now arrive on the evening of the arangetram. There would be no time for the rehearsal that was planned. Instead, my class teacher, Vasantha Vedam, was to arrive by air, in order to help get me ready for the big day.

The tension was palpable. The family flittered tentatively around me. They did not know how to help and what could be done anyway? Fortunately, the big day came by swiftly. The green room at the Bhulabhai Desai Auditorium was quiet—just Vasantha

teacher and me. Not like the busy dressing room at
Kalakshetra before a show, with at least thirty dancers
getting ready for a dance drama. I did my make-up—a
minimal preparation. She helped me with the jewels
and costume. At 6 p.m., in a flurry of excitement,
Sitarama Sharma and Kamala Rani—Rukmini Devi's
two pillars in the concert section, both singers who
also wielded the cymbals—Karaikudi Krishnamurthy,
the grandson of the illustrious veena vaagyakaara
Sambasiva Iyer who played the mridangam, and T. S.
Sankaran, a shishya of the great Mali (Tiruvidaimarudur
Ramaswamy Mahalingam) who played the flute,
entered backstage, hurriedly washed and changed,
were given something to eat, and only just before
going on stage did I get the chance to see them and
seek their blessings. At last, familiar faces! Looking as
grand as they always did for a show, with their pattu
sari and veshtis, kumkum and vibhuti ornamenting
their foreheads. This was the family away from home
that I felt at ease with. I knew all would be well.

Once the chosen compositions began to unfold
in the ritualistic form of a katcheri, time flew by

without a moment for a spare thought. I was grounded into the moves expected of me and, I am told, I delivered without a fuss. No one stood by in the wings—no Mama, no make-up artist, no friend. My compositions were all classics—tried and tested on the hallowed Kalakshetra platform for some decades now— Alarippu in Tisra, the crisp and challenging Kalyani Jatiswaram, the 'Aayar Seriyar' Shabdam, the beautiful Anandabhairavi Varnam 'Sakhiye', a Kshetrayya padam in Kambhoji 'Bala vinave', a Keerthanam 'Nee Uraipai', an Ashtapadi 'Haririha' in Kamarvardhani, a Javali in Kedaram 'Entane varanintu ne', followed by the Bilahari Tillana and a sloka to end the margam as desired by Rukmini Devi. It was a two-and-a-half-hour solo performance stilled only for a brisk ten-minute intermission, for a change of costume. My costumes were not stitched. Either of them. They were draped and could not be called 'costumes'. But they were beautiful kanjeevarams, approved by Athai (Rukmini Devi).

It was only before the last item, the tillana, that I had a hiccup. I went totally, but totally blank. The

musicians had huge smiles upon their faces and had
started to sing the Raga Alapana of the Bilahari
Tillana—a composition of the renowned vaggeyakara,
M. D. Ramanathan who graced our institute with
aplomb. He was first a student and then a teacher
there, continuing to contribute to the richness of
art in the institute. Vasantha teacher came running
from behind the curtain and asked me what I was
waiting for! I said I could not remember my first
move. She showed me a mudra and that was it.
I was on and off before I knew it! We ended with
a Krishna Karnamrita sloka as Rukmini Athai
wished.

Vyjayanthimala, the actress, also one of the greatest
Bharata Natyam dancers of our time, was present, so too
were several senior people from the defence services
and the navy, the British deputy high commissioner,
and a large number of dear friends of the family,
especially of my father, in the audience. Sunoo and
Smita Godrej and, of course, the Swaminathans, with
their daughter, my friend, Indumati. My grandmother's
presence gave me special joy, as also the presence of

my aunts and uncles, cousins, and so many Bombay
friends. It was a memorable evening—one that might
never have been!

1

THE ORIGINS

The prologue of *Malavikagnimitra*, a play written by one of the greatest Sanskrit poets, Kalidasa, describes the contrariness of Shiva's persona thus—

> May the Lord
> who, though enjoying absolute sovereignty from which result many blessings to his votaries, yet himself wears but an elephant-hide;
> who although united in body with his beloved, yet excels the ascetics whose minds are free from the pleasures of the sense;
> in whom there is no pride, although with his eight-fold forms he sustains the universe
> —may he remove your state of ignorance that you may behold the right way.

These varied and contrary facets of the Lord's svabhaavam, or nature, are equally evident in the dance that is said to originate from him. There are truisms about the form we now call Bharata Natyam. But a lot of what we see and hear are difficult to reconcile, including the name itself. Its history, for instance, in the last three hundred years is mired in controversy and confusion. Scholars pontificate along political lines and have exhausted themselves trying to prove what they believe to be the only truth. Some scholars piece together the changes that happened to the dance in social and political terms. Most practitioners, though, especially the great gurus and performers who have ornamented the classical dance form platforms in the last two centuries, have had little to do with these pronouncements. They are made at the high altar of various university programmes in India and abroad. Dancers have preferred to simply dance. And the dance itself has evolved over time and space as it should, quite naturally.

The common thing is to refer to the early-day performer as a devadasi—a handmaiden of God. If you must use a poetic term, then nityasumangali—an ever-auspicious woman—is perhaps more appropriate. Performed simultaneously in the temples, in the courts of kings, and in public for utsavams or festivals, the women who performed at these different venues were different in the training they had, in the kind of compositions they performed, in the compensation they received for their work, as also in their standing in society. The nattuvanar, who was closely associated with the devadasi and even beholden to her largesse in the twentieth century, became the guru of the modern-day dancer by the twenty-first century. Although at one time in history the dancer was the benefactor, a century later their roles were reversed.

I have attempted to capture some salient moments in the course of the history of this dance art through the eighteenth and nineteenth centuries, which contributed to its growth and change over these critical years. It is clear that no one incident is responsible for its variegated journey through time. In fact, multiple occurrences at various levels— political, social, and the upsurge or lack of artistic talent through the decades have guided its destiny. I owe my understanding of these factors and their timeline to keener historians than myself—Jeetendra

Hirschfeld who meticulously researches forgotten histories of the eighteenth century with texts from the Saraswathi Mahal Library in Thanjavur, and also runs Sathir Dance Art, and Venkatakrishnan Sriram whose knowledge of the heritage of the Tamil people is unsurpassed. It was their insights that helped me hone in my fragmented awareness, so typical of the practitioner of the dance. Nandini Ramani's prolific writings on dancers and musicians of yore, their family relationships and particular contributions, were my source for the lives of those who served Bharata Natyam in various capacities, who had their origins in villages and cities all across South India, many of whom migrated to the bigger metropolitan cities at the beginning of the twentieth century. They were related in different ways and branches emerged in places far away from their source, each carrying its own hue and flavour from a remembered culture. I owe all three of them a debt of gratitude for their generosity and indulgence. I have quoted from their notes to me and their published writings.

According to Jeetendra Hirschfeld, 'The 19th

century marks the pivotal period in the social and historical context of Bharata Natyam. It was during this century that the transformation of the dance form, particularly concerning the court repertoire, devadasi system, royal patronage, and colonial influences, significantly shaped its trajectory. While the *Natyashastra* and other texts are integral to Bharata Natyam, this timeline does not delve into them, as it concentrates on the nineteenth-century events that directly influenced the dance's evolution into the twentieth century.'[1]

Art in South India, as in other parts of the country, floundered under British rule, yet flourished in the seventeenth and eighteenth centuries at the largesse of the rulers. Some kings were sensitive to the arts and others, not. Serfoji I, who ruled from 1675–1728, was a patron of the arts and literature in Thanjavur. In relation to dance per se, it was in 1780 that Subbarayan nattuvanar, the son of Gangaimuthu, at the behest of King Tulaja II, began refining the movements and

---

[1] Interview with the author, Chennai, 26 November 2024.

actual adavu system with his father, thus laying a foundation for his own illustrious sons—the Tanjore Quartet, who were the greatest contributors to the form of Bharata Natyam as we now know it, to do what they did in their relatively short lives.

But it was also around this time, in 1784 to be precise, that the law courts headquartered in the three presidencies—Bengal, Madras, and Bombay—summarily classified all dancing girls across the Indian subcontinent as a 'professional' class of public entertainers—a term colonial judges often used as a euphemism for prostitution. The history of dance in present-day teaching at institutions and universities concentrates on the twentieth-century abolishment of the devadasi system, but not on the centuries of ridicule and discrimination that were inflicted upon its practitioners by those who ruled in an earlier period.

In 1798, two significant events took place—the ascension of Tanjore Prince Serfoji II to the throne and the death of Gangaimuthu nattuvanar, grandfather of the Tanjore Quartet. Maharaja Serfoji II embarked on a two-year pilgrimage to Banaras from 1820 to 1822, and upon his return, built his seraglio, the Kalyana Mahal, in Tiruvaiyaru on the banks of the Kaveri River. This marked the beginning of a significant number of dancing girls becoming his sword wives.

In 1824, the advent of the Tanjore Quartet— Chinnayya (1802–56), Ponnayya (1804–64), Sivanandam (1808–63), and Vadivelu (1810–47) at Serfoji II's court, composed dance and music that hugely influenced the repertoire of the South Indian dancer. It would seem as though there is a poetic and even existential justice to their birth and their rather early demise. These brothers reimagined the earlier courtly dances (such as the 'Nirupana Korvai' of Serfoji) into the sequence of compositions that formed, and is till now referred to as, the margam—the 'way'—a repertoire for an evening that begins with an alarippu and ends with a tillana, going through an ocean of physical, emotional, and philosophical drama on the way. This margam is a treasure chest, a gift to any dancer whose destiny it is to perform it. Different schools have an altered order of compositions, especially at the start of the programme, like kauthuvams and pushpanjalis. But the main ingredients have lasted two hundred years. These include the alarippu, jatiswaram, shabdam, swarajathi or varnam, padam, javali, and tillana. There is brilliance not just in the variable nature of these compositions, but a prophetic ingenuity in the order intended for performance. The Quartet were not dancers themselves, but seemingly understood the nature of performance. There is a natural cadence in the compositions that takes one from the physical to the emotional and back to the physical, at first simplistic and then filigreed and complex, moving along at multiple levels simultaneously, when hand-foot coordination is only an 'idea' for a coalescence of the eyes that direct the viewer towards the movement vocabulary, for the shoulders that punctuate the rhythm, for the feet that tap out the inflection of the swaras, for the intelligence of the dancer to simply inform her heart to pay obeisance to her feelings; when lines of demarcation between the limbs, the hastas, and the face and eyes merge into a single statement of love. A movement from the outward to the inward and back. From a gentle warming of the physical to the involvement of the emotional, first in a storytelling mode that is descriptive and outwardly, to an inward and personal level of engagement and admission, only to then return to the abstract, the worldly, the non-personal. These compositions were the vocabulary of every dancer in the twentieth century. And they changed over time to include or eschew certain elements that were thought necessary to do. It is noteworthy that the swarajathi as a composition appeared as early as the latter part of the eighteenth century, only to be sometimes replaced by the latter-day pada-varnam as a key virtuosic dance piece.

In 1829, the illustrious Quartet had a falling out with the king, Serfoji II, and left the Thanjavur court. History is fascinating, for if these brothers had not left Thanjavur, the seat of great happenings in dance and music, their talent and influence would not have spread to other illustrious courts such as Travancore and Mysore. It would surely have put a small dent in Maharaja Swati Tirunal's prolific indulgence of compositions, for they came to his court with their own bagful of gems.

Soon after, in 1832, Maharaja Serfoji II passed away. Shivaji II (who would come to be called Maharaja Shivaji), aged only twenty-four, was coronated that year. Ponnayya and Sivanandam returned to the Thanjavur court under Maharaja Shivaji. Chinnayya, however, remained in Mysore and Vadivelu in Travancore.

The birth of Princess Vijaya Mohana Muktamba in 1845 marked a pivotal moment in Thanjavur's cultural and social transitions. But only ten years later, on 29 October 1855, Maharaja Shivaji passed away, leaving behind seventeen widows, forty-two seraglio wives, and thirteen children. But, ironically, no recognized male heir! In 1856, the British East India Company rejected Princess Vijaya Mohana's right to succession, declaring the Thanjavur kingdom extinct.

By 1860, Thomas B. Macaulay's Indian Penal Code (IPC) was implemented, standardizing criminal law across India under British rule. While intended to modernize legal systems, it also imposed colonial values, criminalizing traditional practices that conflicted with British norms. This had significant implications for communities like the devadasis.

As for the rulers of Thanjavur, after a seven-year legal battle, the British East India Company returned the palace estate and private property to the dowager Kamakshi Bai and the royal family in 1862. However, they declined to revisit the question of succession to the Thanjavur throne. Despite this setback, Kamakshi Bai and Princess Vijaya Mohana devoted years of tireless effort to restoring the kingdom's cultural dignity. They preserved the traditions of the royal court, maintaining its grandeur and influence well into the late nineteenth century.

Princess Vijaya Mohana Muktamba died in 1885 at the age of forty and soon after her, in 1892, the dowager Kamakshi Bai passed away, signalling the final collapse of the Thanjavur kingdom.

On 17 December 1875, a most curious incident occurred when Tanjore Gnyana (1857–1922) performed for Prince Edward of Wales and the elite of the British Raj as well as dignitaries of the Madras Presidency at the Madras Royapuram Railway Station. By virtue of her journey from temple dancing to performing in venues such as durbars, reading rooms, garden parties, and this most unusual, yet formal venue, 'Gnyana served as an allegory that reflected the cultural shift under colonial influence. Her performances in these modern spaces, including the grand event at Royapuram Railway Station, symbolize the blending of Indian tradition with colonial modernity. This event, featuring innovations like electric lighting and a performance stage, highlights how colonialism reshaped and modernized cultural practices.'[2]

With the establishment of the High Court of Madras in 1862, civil cases concerning the devadasis were admitted. Between 1862 and 1889, multiple judgements, often contradictory, were passed. Some distinguished between the devadasis and prostitutes, others did not, causing the Indian Penal Code to forbid prostitution of minors, but not bringing the adoption of girls by devadasis into its ambit.

In 1881, social reformer and scholar Kandukuri Veeresalingam Pantulu launched a campaign against

---

[2]Jeetendra Hirschfeld/ Sathir Dance Art Trust.

the devadasi system, which can be considered the birth of the anti-nautch movement. He submitted a memorandum to Governor Lord Wenlock in 1883, equating nautch girls with prostitutes, and requested the governor and government officials to avoid events where these women were allowed to present their art. By 1909, the Mysore government, a major benefactor, stopped availing the services of devadasis in state-controlled temples.

The formation of the Indian National Congress in 1885 marked the rise of organized anti-colonial activism. Be that as it may, in 1887 Queen Victoria's Golden Jubilee was celebrated in the Madras Presidency when hundreds of nautch parties were held throughout the presidency—the last of its kind on that scale.

The International Oriental Arts Movement sprouted in the 1890s, led by eminent figures such as Rabindranath Tagore, Ananda Coomaraswamy, Swami Vivekananda, Annie Besant, and Ernest Havell. They sought to revive and reimagine Indian art and culture. Their efforts celebrated India's artistic heritage while challenging colonial dismissals of its value, laying the groundwork for a more modern appreciation of Bharata Natyam.

The 1890s also saw the rise of the anti-nautch social reform movement led by Veeresalingam Pantulu, Venkataratnam Naidu, and Periyar (as E. V. Ramasamy was referred to), and later reformers like Moovalur Ramamirtham—a Tamil social reformer and political activist who campaigned against the devadasi system, viewing it as exploitative and morally corrupt. The movement gained momentum a few decades later with the support of the social reformer Muthulakshmi Reddy, whose own mother Chandrammal was a devadasi—who at the age of eleven years had implored Narayanaswami to become her patron, thereby extricating her from the system. British officials like Macaulay, whose policies had earlier shaped social attitudes towards the devadasis along with Dr Muthulakshmi Reddy's efforts, contributed to social reform and women's rights in colonial India.

By 1911, driven by these social reformers and changing societal attitudes, a boycott of performances by devadasis emerged, as the entire system came under increased scrutiny. This marked a turning point in the perception of the devadasi tradition, leading to its eventual decline and the transformation of the form into a redefined cultural practice.

The publication of Katherine Mayo's *Mother India* in 1927 resulted in a massive debate in the Central Legislative Assembly on the devadasi system. The debate was initiated by V. Ramadas Pantulu of Madras. Interestingly, this was opposed by Law Member S. R. Das as the government did not consider a devadasi to be the same as a prostitute. In 1927, the Madras Legislative Council also took up a discussion on Dr Muthulakshmi Reddy's resolution to abolish the devadasi system, but in 1928, the debate taken up in the first session ended with a request that the proposed bill be withdrawn like the sister resolution in the Central Legislature. On 3 November 1928, the Association of Devadasis of Madras Presidency was formed to counter this. Their appeal was drafted and circulated among devadasis in various temples in the Madras Presidency. Dr Muthulakshmi Reddy then proposed an amendment to the Madras Hindu

Religious Endowments Act to stop dedication of girls to temples and to deed over to the devadasis, the lands they held by virtue of their service.

On 4 November 1928, Dr Reddy moved a resolution that the Madras Legislative Council request the government to undertake legislation to stop the practice of dedicating young girls and women to temples. On 10 November 1928, the Law Member, Sir C. P. Ramaswami Aiyar asked the devadasis to submit a fuller memorandum, which they did on 11 November 1928. The final memorandum was presented to the Law Member on 23 November 1928. In 1929, the Act was passed. In essence, it was what Dr Muthulakshmi Reddy had proposed in September 1928. But it was only on 26 November 1947, with the help of Gandhiji, that the Madras Devadasi (Prevention of Dedication) Bill 1947 was passed.

Jeetendra Hirschfeld states with utmost clarity what other historians refuse to admit: 'The devadasi's history is fraught with dilemmas and paradoxes. It is not a history of clear or precise answers but one that is complex and fragmented. Her story resists simple, binary interpretations and remains an unsolvable narrative, full of friction and ambiguity.'

It was under lawyer, dancer, critic, and cultural reformer E. Krishna Iyer's guidance that on 15 March 1931, the Music Academy that had been founded a few years earlier in 1928, organized the very first public performance of dance in a non-religious or non-royal court setting. It was by the Kalyani sisters— Rajalakshmi and Jeevaratnam, daughters of Kalyani Ammal of Thiruvalaputhur. On 3 January 1932, a second public performance of dance under the auspices of the Music Academy was presented by Mylapore Gowri, a well-known devadasi of the time.

In 1932, the raja of Bobbili, R. S. Ramakrishna Ranga Rao, was elected premier of Madras, and Kumararaja M. A. Muthiah Chettiar became mayor of the Corporation of Madras. Interestingly, a nautch party was held on this occasion. The firebrand Dr Muthulakshmi Reddy, who had resigned from the Council in 1930 following Gandhi's call for Satyagraha, wrote scathing letters to *The Hindu*, which prompted equally emphatic rejoinders from E. Krishna Iyer. The debate was out in the open and talked about.

In January 1933, the third public performance organized by the Music Academy saw not only the exceptional talent of the Kalyani sisters once again, but also focused on the question of the nautch in their annual conference. It was to this concert that Yagnaraman escorted his twenty-nine-year-old sister Rukmini Shastri, who the world would come to know as Rukmini Devi Arundale. In her own words, she left absolutely enchanted! Today, the world of dancers of this form know too well that it was her very enchantment with it that changed the norm of the time, and would grant each of us of future generations the license to learn a very beautiful dance art.

2

SCHOOLS AND STYLES

There are two people, born two centuries apart, who may be attributed and rightly acknowledged with creating and then recreating the form of Bharata Natyam as we now know it. Not the repertoire, not the rituals of the temple. They occupied themselves not with the teaching or performing of dance, as much as with conceiving and creating an actual pedagogy of the form. What is it? That integral, intrinsic detail that ultimately leads to the expression of it. That which could be taught, that which would become the bedrock of technique upon which the style would express itself. The first was Gangaimuthu nattuvanar, grandfather of the Tanjore Quartet, who died in 1798, the year that Tanjore Prince Serfoji II ascended the throne, and the other was Rukmini Devi. They lived during the eighteenth and twentieth centuries, respectively. Each did in their own time what was necessary to enhance the pedagogy of the form and draw attention to its intrinsic beauty. He was from within the system, and she brought to it the vision of the future world it would occupy.

Between them, in the year 1869, a man was born outside the royal palace who would emerge as a pivotal figure among the nattuvanars—the traditional teachers of the dance. Born in a small village called Pandanallur in Thanjavur, his name became synonymous with that of his village. He was named Meenakshisundaram Pillai, an icon of the nattuvanar lineage of the twentieth century. He trained numerous nattuvanars and devadasis. His most illustrious disciples were the hereditary Pandanallur Jayalakshmi (1930–2017), Ram Gopal (1912–2003), Rukmini Devi (1904–86), and Mrinalini Sarabhai (1918–2016)—all of whom became icons of the Pandanallur style of Bharata Natyam, although their interpretation of it, as also their individual contribution to the field, varied substantially. His own family continued his legacy and this also took on varying shades of interpretation.

The Pandanallur bani or style is distinguished by gurus of integrity, quiet, yet proud demeanours, who transferred their sotthu or 'wealth' of knowledge of the dance, with pride. Well known among this illustrious family of nattuvanars were Chokkalingam Pillai, foremost among his disciples, who at first assisted the doyen and was later appointed as a vaadyar (being a teacher) in Kalakshetra, along with Dhandayuthapani Pillai. Subbaraya Pillai, who was Chokkalingam Pillai's son, taught Alarmel Valli, Meenakshi Chittaranjan, and others, and Swaminatha Pillai taught and did nattuvangam (teacher and one who leads a team of musicians by wielding the cymbals) for numerous dancers in Delhi, like myself. These two brought a heightened dignity and authenticity to their teaching, as also to their nattuvangam, serving the Pandanallur bani with distinction.

Rukmini Devi learnt the form diligently from the doyen, Meenakshisundaram Pillai, and two years later, at the Diamond Jubilee Convention of the Theosophical Society in December 1935, she presented a traditional margam in the coveted style that had till then belonged to the devadasi, excluding anyone outside the community. Opposition to her performance was pronounced, but she was protected by the Theosophical Society, inhabited then by thinkers, poets, educationalists, and freedom fighters, world citizens—whose opinion was not biased by religion or caste. They lauded her engagement with one of India's finest dance arts and applauded her effort. Their minds turned to education. India was on the brink of Independence and she and others like her wished to see a return to India's gurukula form of education. The elite in India had bought into the British public school system with forms of punishment that were alien to Indian teaching systems. An 'education without fear', 'art without vulgarity', and 'beauty without cruelty' became Rukmini Devi's goals for life.

A month later, on 6 January 1936, she established the International Academy of Arts, which was later renamed Kalakshetra in Madras (as Chennai was then known). Scholars were put on the job, old texts disseminated, elderly musicians and dancers engaged, a gurukulam created under the trees, and children enrolled from among the families living in Adyar, a neighbourhood in south Chennai. The art would be passed down. It was too beautiful to be kept under wraps for the entertainment of privileged men alone. Kalakshetra—what a revolutionary story that was!

On 30 May 1913, Thanjavur K. P. Kittappa, a renowned nattuvanar and custodian of Bharata Natyam's rich heritage, was born. A direct descendant of the Tanjore Quartet, Kittappa played a pivotal role in preserving the art form's legacy. He had a close association with his maternal grandfather, Meenakshisundaram Pillai, and from the 1940s, alongside his father K. Ponnaiah (1883–1945) and brother K. P. Sivanandam (1917–2003), began documenting the music and dance compositions of the Tanjore Quartet and their predecessors. He was a grand master of the form, a singer who knew the nuances of the songs for dance, a brilliant nattuvanar, a loved acharya (teacher), and one who greatly contributed to the legacy of his forefathers. These book publications made what was previously preserved through oral transmission accessible to dance teachers and practitioners worldwide. This monumental effort ensured the survival and dissemination of Bharata

Natyam's repertoire. The year 2024 marked the bicentenary of the Tanjore Quartet's emergence as royal court composers, highlighting their enduring impact on Bharata Natyam.

Another nattuvanar who embellished the Pandanallur bani was C. Subbaraya Pillai, the son of Chokkalingam Pillai. Yet another leading name was Karaikkal Natesan Dhandayuthapani Pillai, who belonged to a lineage of traditional nadaswaram players of Karaikal. He joined the dance orchestra of Kalakshetra as a musician to assist Chokkalingam Pillai while he trained students of the dance. After he strode out on his own career path, Dhandayuthapani Pillai further fermented his name on the field as a composer of great merit and a nattuvanar who had no equal at the time. I remember accompanying Karaikudi R. Krishnamurthy for a performance of the actress Jayalalithaa, who was at the height of her popularity. He made me sit behind him only to observe the great nattuvanar. He was so proud to play mridangam for Dhandayuthapani Pillai's concerts, as very few others could at the time. Such was his prowess! He

had illustrious disciples in Srividya, the daughter of
M. L. Vasanthakumari, Vennira Adai Nirmala, and
Jayalalithaa, later to become the chief minister of
Tamil Nadu—all of whom were famous actresses in
the film industry of Tamil Nadu. Apart from them,
there was Jayalakshmi Alva in Mangalore, and other
leading stars like Waheeda Rehman and Asha Parekh.
Usha Srinivasan and Urmila Satyanarayana carry
on his special legacy. Dhandayuthapani's brother,
Dakshinamurthi Pillai, taught in Delhi and Pakkirisamy
Pillai taught in Mumbai.

Tanjore Balasaraswati, born on 9 February 1918,
was a pre-eminent Bharata Natyam icon, celebrated for
her artistry and rootedness in the devadasi heritage.
She was also a staunch follower of the Thanjavur bani.
Her lineage was impeccable. She was the daughter of
T. Jayammal, the grand-daughter of Veena Dhanammal,
and a disciple of Tanjore Kandappa Pillai, who
was himself a descendant of the Tanjore Quartet.
Her sensitive musical knowledge, derived from her
grandmother Dhanammal, was beautifully embellished
on stage by several illustrious musicians over the

years, among them her own mother Jayammal, her aunt Lakshmiratnammal, her cousins T. Brinda and T. Mukta, C. P. Gnanasundaram, T. Vishwanathan— also a grandson of Dhanammal who sang for her and later accompanied her on the flute—and by T. Ranganathan, another brother, on the mridangam. It was this knowledge that impressed her ability to emote sensitively in the expressional aspect of the dance, something that became her forte. She was comfortable in that genre and excelled in it.

The family was understandably covetous, reluctant to share their high art. Apart from her daughter, Lakshmi, who started learning rather late, her grandson Aniruddha Knight, and a handful of loving disciples—Priyamvada and Nandini, both daughters of Dr V. Raghavan—and her American students Luise Scripps, Kay Poursine, Aggie Brenneman, and a few others, the lineage is rich, yet lean. However, what is not noticeable in numbers is hugely compensated for by admirers of her dance. There is no dearth amongst many present-day exponents of those who admired her and deeply loved her art, especially those amongst us who had the privilege of witnessing her dance.

Through the 1930s, several dancers emerged from the Pandanallur tradition. Jayalakshmi Nachiyar was a brilliant dancer, who married the raja of Ramnad, Shanmugha Rajeswara Sethupathi, a patron of the arts, and lived in Mylapore, Madras. It is said that she was the first traditional dancer to have her musicians seated on the dais, as opposed to standing behind her on stage. Perhaps she had taken a leaf out of Rukmini Devi's performance in 1935, when this change had been executed. She was not the only dancer of standing that emerged from that bani. Pandanallur Sabharanjitham was also featured in the Music Academy in 1936 and had accompanied her guru, Meenakshisundaram Pillai, when he came to Adyar to teach Rukmini Devi.

Jeevaratnam and Rajalakshmi danced between 1950 and 1965, both grand-daughters of Thiruvalaputhur Kalyani Ammal, herself an illustrious exponent of the Pandanallur bani. The former was a talented dancer, who was kept from being dedicated to the temple by her mother, thus allowing her a career in Madras. Her father was a Congressman who encouraged her talent and stood firm that she should not fall victim to social customs. He disallowed her from getting into films, which was a lucrative trend then among dancers.

P. Ranganayaki was another dancer, dedicated to the temple at the age of seventeen. She maintained her tradition of ritualistic songs and dances. Dr Saskia Kersenboom was a senior student of Parampara and worked with Ranganayaki to create a production called 'Devadasi Murai—Remembering Devadasis'. It also resulted in Saskia's PhD dissertation 'Nityasumangali: Devadasi Tradition of South India'—the first-ever documentation of the by-gone traditions of the devadasis.

The Mysore school of Bharata Natyam is remembered by Kadur Venkatalakshamma, who was born in 1906 and was the last representative of the Mysore palace tradition. She served the court of Raja Nalvadi Krishna Raja Wadiyar for thirty years. She had the privilege of dancing for both the coronation and the wedding ceremony of Sri Jayachamaraja Wadiyar, a patron of the arts, Sanskrit, and literature. She even served as the head of the dance department of the University of Mysore.

One of the most reputed styles of Bharata Natyam is the Vazhuvur bani, made illustrious by its foremost teacher, Vazhuvoor Ramaiah Pillai. Kamala Lakshman was his prime disciple, whose elegance on stage brought laurels to the style. Amidst this male-dominated guru parampara (lineage of teachers), there emerged K. J. Sarasa, a woman who became prominent among the teachers in Madras for over five decades. She was trained under Kattumannar Koil Muthukumara Pillai in Mayavaram, where she witnessed the arangetram of Kumari Kamala. Vazhuvoor Ramaiah Pillai visited Mayavaram, saw her in this school or silamba koodam as it was then called, and brought her to Madras in 1945. It was he who encouraged her to become a nattuvanar, taking her with him to the rehearsals of several star dancers like Vyjayanthimala and Kumari Kamala. She was also a cousin of K. N. Dhandayuthapani Pillai, who was himself making waves as a brilliant nattuvanar. Her very first disciple was Rathna Papa.

Thanjavur Kamalambal was another dancer who captivated audiences of Ramanathapuram, Thanjavur, and Seithur. Her style was passed on to her niece, Mythili, wife of T. K. Kalyanasundaram of Mumbai. Kalyanasundaram was the son of T. P. Kuppiah Pillai and learnt his art from Mahalingam Pillai, Kuppiah Pillai's brother, whose ancestors were patronized and honoured by the royal durbars of Baroda, Mysore, and Ramanathapuram. The family settled in Bombay in 1945 and trained generations of dancers at their established school—Rajarajeswari Bharata Natya Kala Mandir.

A self-effacing addition to the illustrious line of male gurus was a middle-aged woman, Kalanidhi Narayanan. A revered teacher of abhinaya, who performed as a young girl under the nattuvanar Dhanamanikkam, as also under K. Ganesan, son of Kandappa Pillai, she was a disciple of Kannappa Pillai of Kanchipuram, Gowri Ammal, and Chinniah Naidu, and learnt music, specifically padams, from Kamakshiammal, daughter of Veena Dhanammal. Kalanidhi mami put this very early training to informed use after a hiatus of three decades or more for marriage and children. And what an amazing contribution she made to the world of dance after that, in the form of video recordings, books, and workshops. Apart from her devoted students in Chennai, she travelled to major cities like Delhi, Mumbai, and Bangalore, and taught other seekers the art of abhinaya. Her disciples continue her rich tradition.

A host of dancers emerged from these various schools and vaadyars. Vyjayanthimala, a veteran of the K. P. Kittappa Pillai school, in spite of an illustrious foray into films, has stayed firm to this day to the traditional principles of the form, exuding a joy and internal connect to her dance that is astounding.

In 1950, the Serfoji Saraswati Mahal Archive in Thanjavur was reclaimed by the Indian state as a national archive. The library, a repository of manuscripts, was reorganized and began to function as an Orientalist archive. In the 1950s, the Indian state also recognized South Indian Carnatic music and dance, which had flourished and reached their pinnacle in the Thanjavur courts, as among the nation's classical art forms. By the 1960s, Bharata Natyam was seen as India's quintessential dance in cultural exchange programmes with the West.

Its exponents were many, representing every branch of the single tree.

3

TECHNIQUES AND SYMBOLISM

$\int$ankara Menon, a teacher I greatly admired, said: 'Man expresses himself both as an individual and as a member of the community of men. As the individual, he moves towards the realization of the aloneness of the self and, in his communal aspect, his progress is towards the realization and inclusion of all creation within himself. Both these aspects are vital. The integration of the personality alone permits the growth of a contented society.' For me as an artist, this is apparent everyday—the need to grow from within, as also the relevance and effect of what you do upon those around you. Individual growth happens within the context of the larger society that we live in.

As a dancer, I love the solo format, which is what I was trained for. As a choreographer, I have grown to love the interaction of bodies and minds that happens in ensembles. I would wish to dance with my soul, like Isadora Duncan. My attempt is to be moved by the sahitya or verse like a Sufi saint is, who sees and reads the philosophy behind the metaphors. I wish to be swayed by the melody and cadence of the music like a bird that feels the changing mood of the wind under its wings. I also want to feel the space around me, not by looking at it and assessing it, but with my eyes closed, in my mind's eye, my feet making contact with the floor upon which I move, while I disappear into a world of make-believe in my head. What I am sadly conscious of, though, is that I must do these things in the presence of others, with watchful eyes that analyse my every move, that wish to partake, that sit in judgement of, that critique the viability of what you do with societal and sometimes traditional norms. This inner and outer reality very rarely find balance in the artist. There is often nothing to bridge the gap between how you feel and how others feel about you, or your work. One reality is often incompatible with the other. Norms are applied that belong either to the past, or follow present-day trends and mannerisms— neither of these is where my own consciousness lies.

When you learn the traditional arts, there are, it

seems, two ways to do so. One is to ask no questions and simply listen. This method is useful, for it allows for a keener listening and although many questions remain unanswered, an interesting other thing grows in you—a non-judgmental attitude that people in our field would call 'humility'. Bhakti or devotion, shraddha or effort, and sadhana or contemplative practice are words that we grow with in the arts in India. This does not mean that we know what they mean or denote in practice. You simply grow up accepting and absorbing through years of confused parroting and later, having soaked in almost more than you can handle, you spend the rest of your life discovering what the teaching actually meant. And it is lovely, because you arrive upon the truth in your own time. It almost seems as though you discovered it! The other way is to ask questions at every step of the way, which often serves to confuse you and sometimes the teacher too! And in the bargain, the subject under scrutiny gets side-tracked. Egos begin their macabre dance.

The ancients placed tremendous emphasis on the

development of memory. Modern educators condemn committing things to memory and especially learning by rote. Mere photographic retentiveness, they opine, is not good memory. It is a 'creative' assimilation of the educational content of a matter that is good memory. If something is committed to memory, the knowledge so committed must become part of the personality, part of the individual self. In dance and music, artists have to remember a large repository of compositions, learnt over years of regular practice. This memory of beautiful verse, ancient melodies, and movement patterns is worked on until it becomes part of one's nature. You stand at the heart of the learning. It is the growth of your own body, mind, and soul that is the point of the learning process, not the passing of exams or the acquisition of degrees. It is your individuality, your culture, and the climate of awareness about you that gives the composition its character. The arts, in this sense, have played a critical role in addressing complex issues in personality development and well-being. The arts have advanced values by tapping into the aesthetic and imaginative capacity of the child.

Logic and science are a relief from this creative world, though sometimes a burden.

Starting early has its advantages in sports and the arts. In the classical dance traditions, an early start around the age of six or seven helps the body and mind to wrap itself around what can be complex configurations and demanding, non-compromising discipline. Physical pain is not an issue at this age. The teacher's severity and strictness is most of the time appreciated, as long as it is consistent and there is a sprinkling of appreciation or the crack of a smile from time to time. Children love routine and know intrinsically that they are learning something special.

Correcting technique until a movement becomes an extension of who you are, is the bedrock of good dancing. Two years spent exclusively on learning adavus or movement-based phrases that each include specific footwork, hand movements that compliment them, ornamented by hasta mudras or hand gestures, head and eye contact with the above, and strong and soft, steely and playful body movements and finding ways to make each of these speak to each other in your own particular way, pays huge dividends and saves many heartaches trying to correct some tiny detail later. The mandalas, which are the basic postures of the body that define Bharata Natyam, are the araimandi or half-sitting posture, the sthanaka, the muramandi, the swastika, etc. These postures are the frame or grid of the style. They cannot be assumed to be easy. Exercises that help different body types to achieve these postures and arrive upon them in a second, as required in different movement patterns, must be done to help understand the demand of each one of them. Sitting or standing, knees bent or stretched, using the swastika or not, weight forward or back—these mandalas must become as comfortable as sitting or standing is. The difference is that sitting or standing in dance is without the support of walls or chairs! As severe and particular as you can be in strictly adhering to these mandalas in the beginning of your training, that much ease is to be had in the unadulterated edifice that is built upon them.

The adavus, which could be static in one place,

to those that move you to the sides and around you, to those that require you to fall to the ground with different parts of the body touching the floor at different moments, to those that lift you above the ground in short sharp jabs, longer leaps or high jumps, and to movements that rotate you around your axis called brahmaris, all these have to be mastered, slowly and meticulously. At first, in regular time cycles like chatushra which is the universal four-beat time cycle, but then in all the five jaatis.

The five jaatis are not referred to enough by teachers in the early stages of learning. The four-beat cycle is used ad nauseam in early learning, which is understandable, as it has a square, block-like repetitive nature that can be divided easily, and even those with a bad sense of timing tend to get this 'even' number. The other four are all 'odd' numbers—tishram or three, khandam or five, mishram or seven, and sankeernam or nine. Together they cover all the numbers that exist. But dividing or doubling an odd number is necessary to arrive at different speeds and this is not only difficult, but also requires an obsession or indulgence to master them enough, to seem as though dancing to the odd beat is as simple as dancing to chatushra. In my book, the earlier the better to introduce and practice the pancha jaatis.

In the Kalakshetra school of Bharata Natyam, there are at least a hundred such adavus or movement patterns that have now become the 'textbook', the pedagogy of learning the form. It was not so in the beginning. Swaminatha Pillai from Pandanallur, a descendent of that very bani that inspired Rukmini Devi to learn and propagate it, said that the adavus were only a handful when he was in his youth, sitting behind the illustrious doyen of that family, Meenakshisundaram Pillai, watching him teach. This was so even when Rukmini learnt the art form from him. It was her own dissemination of the form that allowed her to re-create an enhanced pedagogy based upon what she had learnt, no doubt, but which soon multiplied and became the syllabus that was taught in Kalakshetra. It was a gradual evolution of stance and movement and a logical development, an unfolding of levels of understanding. A strong foundation is the hallmark of the Kalakshetra school. This is where she made the first difference to Bharata Natyam.

As far as abstract dance of this nature, that which we call nritta, is concerned, practice makes perfect. Repetition is valuable beyond question. The little gems of understanding the movement and feeling happen when an adavu is repeated again and again, a thousand times, not only at different speeds but also in the different jaatis, and then in combination with other adavus that occur just before or after it, in the different choreographies. Varying movement patterns have to become part of the dancer's body memory. Ultimately, though, no teacher or mirror can tell you if a movement is right. You have to feel it and know it to be true or false. Slipping and losing your balance are overt examples of incorrect technique. In actual fact, imperfection is far more subtle and, therefore, very difficult to pinpoint, teach, or correct. Every muscle in the body plays a part in delivering a movement, including the brain and the heart. At some point in the learning curve, a dancer has to take ownership from the teacher and make the dance his or her own expression and have a good reason to defend every interpretation of what was learnt, perhaps, in a rather orthodox manner.

For instance, while living in Delhi I was invited to perform solo at Kalakshetra. At the end of the programme, I chose to present a tillana composed by the violin maestro, Lalgudi G. Jayaraman in the raga Revati that I had choreographed. In the mai adavu section, I turned to face the back of the stage—a motif that repeated itself a few times in the composition. After the show, Periya Sarada, who was the oldest teacher at Kalakshetra, asked if I would come and see her at six o'clock the next morning at the Theosophical Society, where she resided, for a 'debriefing'. I went, as asked. There had been numerous times when I was a student that this had happened after a show, especially if I had played a lead role. She opened her tiny book of handwritten notes and among her points of both praise and critique, was the question of my 'unorthodox' turning of the back to the audience and staying like that for a few seconds more than was the norm at the time. I explained that the proscenium stage was partial to frontal viewing. I questioned this, as well as the idea that an offering or respectful adherence to the audience presumed that the God of the stage resided in that direction only. She wasn't amused. But when I said 'thank goodness it was me and no one else' who performed this anomaly, she asked why. I said it was because I had a leaner 'behind' than most other dancers! That made her laugh and we agreed to disagree on that point.

The compositions in Bharata Natyam that you learn after the initial years of 'grinding', no matter which bani or school you come from, can be dated to at least two to three hundred years ago. They were exquisite compositions. And when this happens, even with a simple Saveri jatiswaram, a whole new set of challenges and things to work on occupies your mind and body. A new and unexpected frustration becomes a sthayi bhava or underlying feeling during this stage of learning. But the compositions themselves, you can have no truck with. Among them, those that already existed before the Tanjore Quartet were the mallaris, kauvthuvams, and thevarams that were performed in the temples, intrinsic to temple rituals and mandatory celebrations of particular deities on days sacred to each of them. The navasandhi kauvthuram is an example of these and is still known to dancers like the doyen Vyjayanthimala Bali and Narthaki Natarajan, both disciples of Kittappa Pillai. There were also compositions from the beautiful kuravanjis of the time, popularly performed during festivals, when people flocked to see the hunter and the gypsy fortune-teller's story, both of whom were well-loved characters. At a later date, these older compositions ran parallel to the new jatiswarams, shabdams, varnams, padams, and tillanas that were composed by the Tanjore Quartet as part of the new margam that they so brilliantly conceived of for the new age dancer who was not privy to the ritualistic compositions performed by the nityasumangalis. What would they perform then? The Quartet had the answer. Whether one or two hundred years old, what these brothers created has proved to be an exquisite alternative for those that are from 'the outside'. These are not poor alternatives. They are to be learnt with diligence. Each of the nattuvanars coveted their family repertoire and taught it only when the student was fit for it. Their expectation was not merely in your being able to remember it, but in your capacity to carry it forward with respect and correct adherence to their wishes, on to the stage and into the future. The composition must be acknowledged with a debt of gratitude to the lineage of artists who have performed it before you.

Abhinaya, the second important aspect of the form, came upon me quietly, almost surreptitiously. It simply happened one fine day, and while my grip over this exalted repertoire of nritta compositions was getting to be somewhat stable by this point of my learning, the inability to cope with the new and relatively small padam threw me completely! I believe that some of us never really get over the shock of it. As a result, many dancers hardly perform them and when they do, they deal with the nayika rather uncomfortably. Thankfully, there are more exceptions to that rule now than there were in the 1960s and 70s, when brilliance had become the highest virtue.

In the classical solo tradition, especially in the all-

important varnam, padams, javalis, and viruttams, a
nayika or heroine is more often than not, the narrator.
But this is gradually and surely changing. There are
more male dancers in the field now, who prefer
narrative compositions that tell a story, perhaps from
mythology—with characterization and conversations
between characters that move the story along. Some
of them are interesting new interpretations of ancient
tales. This is definitely more appealing to audiences.
But it does take away from the centrality of the 'self',
which is what compositions like the varnams, padams,
and javalis allowed for.

It is also significant that the persona of the human
soul is the one who tells the story of life. It is she who
explains the vagaries of life, the trials of existence.
She does not deny her weakness or her vulnerability.
There is great comfort in the knowledge that one
is with blemish. That way the search continues and
growth is possible. In fact, a complete change of
personality is within one's reach—in a lifetime of being
tossed about on the waters of relationships. What is
portrayed in the classical solo format is then perhaps

the search of the self, by the self. The beloved is a metaphor for that which we seek. In each of us this goal is different, but always beckoning, just beyond reach. With some it remains physical, for a few it is an intellectual pursuit, for others an overwhelming emotional journey. The nayika, on the other hand, simply says, 'If you come to me, seek refuge in me, you will find true happiness.'

But not without her first accusing, abusing, lamenting, accosting, seducing. It is she who bites the dust. But it is also she who revels in the glory. It is she who looks at the story square in the face. She uses no props, no costume, nor any devices to say it. She says it with tears, with anger, with jealousy, with regret, with heartbreak.

She says it simply as it is. For what other way is there, after all, to tell a story?

ſ

For over five centuries, Telugu, the lyrical language of Andhra Pradesh, was profusely and deftly used by composers to write for dance. The musical form of the padam, some say akin to the thumri in Hindustani sangeet, has the melodic structure of the composition and the raga blends aesthetically and often seamlessly with the verse. The padam is set in a slow tempo, the slowness allowing for a rasa or sentiment to be established. Virtuosity in speed and form are not an asset when doing these padams. What is required here is extreme patience and thehrav, the ability to hold an idea and stay with it. No wonder it is still a thing of rare achievement that every dancer seeks to accomplish. A padam is an unchartered path of self-discovery. To find a lyric that appeals to you, to relate to the music of it, to fathom its depth and the caves of hidden meaning and possibilities within—these are the joys of rendering these verses through dance. For the rasika or viewer too, it is a journey of discovery and one that takes a lifetime of listening and watching to appreciate.

These particular poets were not ascetics running away from life, but lovers of life who took the other route to liberation, through life! It is interesting that the classical poetic traditions were penned predominantly by men and it is the persona of the 'woman' or the nayika through whom the story of life is reflected and narrated. Perhaps men recognized a woman's vulnerability and tenacity to be a symbol of a constantly questioning and evolving mind. The nayika or heroine addresses her ramblings to the nayaka or hero, or alternatively to the sakhi or friend. It is a common misconception that the subject matter of the dance in India in the so-called classical genre is the man–woman relationship and the travails and joys of that relationship—the yearning, the pining, the misunderstanding, the incompleteness, etc. On the contrary, it is my understanding after living with these arts for a lifetime, that this construct is a brilliant theatrical ploy. The nayika does not represent the voice of the woman, but the jiva atma—man, woman, or other. The dialogue between the jiva atma, the human soul, and param atma, the divine soul, between that which is apparent and that which is a mystery, continues endlessly and without answer. Sex and love are an essential part of life and so a part of our poetry, as also part of our prayer. Spiritualism is equally essential in the Indian context. It is the madhura-bhakti of the poet, the musician, and the dancer which is the highest form of worship, one that acknowledges the oneness of the universe, of man and God. In this sense, it is the woman who best represents the ever-journeying soul, without bias to sex, full of human frailty and hope. She never tires of questioning, seeking answers, finding comfort in small slivers of wisdom that become apparent through introspection and faith.

To achieve excellence and poise in the abstract expression of movement with technique, speed, accuracy, grace, and a joie de vivre is a delight to watch. To see an artist's deep involvement in the expression of feelings and nuanced moods is rarer and when present, it can be frittered away on stories about the hero, the nayaka. One often feels that the nayika is lost, forgotten. What is her story?

Along with these skills, an empathetic and sensitive ear for music and an innate, natural sense of rhythm are gifts we receive in our genetic make-up. Without them, a dancer can only limp along helplessly. A technical, analytical knowledge of the dance and being able to theorize dance practice is the bane of our lives. A disdain and even suspicion between scholarship and practice is healthy.

4

COSTUME AND ATTIRE

$\mathcal{I}$t was the dancers and musicians of yesteryears who seem to have set the tone for trends in dressing and attire in different social milieu. The jewellery and costumes that draped and shaped the body of the dancer were particular to different time periods. What they chose to sheathe their bodies in on stage was and is important, if not vital, as this continues to be their public demeanour and their personal expression.

In South India, the villages around Kancheepuram produced the finest silk saris for the deities in the temple, as also for the public. Typically, a woman possessed only a couple of these exquisite six-yard saris that were part of her dowry when she married. She did not need more, for they lasted a lifetime and were not treasured away, but worn daily. They were not meant to be passed on to daughters, but to be worn soft through decades of wifely and motherly duties, till you could not tell the person from the garment. We all have vivid memories of what our mothers and grandmothers wore, but in my case, especially what my guru wore. These memories hone in our own preferences, but also give the dance form we practice, a special character. Having said that, it is not as though adherence to the form and textile associated with a particular dance or musical form is an indicator of good dance or music.

In the early part of the twentieth century, the dancer wore what the deity in the temple was draped with. She wore the colours of Parvati and Lakshmi, of Saraswathi and Andal, of Valli and Devayani. Parrot greens and leaf greens, the colour of the rice fields in the Thanjavur district; deep purples and baingani purples; arakku, a deep maroon; reds, the colours of the kumkumam worn by women on their foreheads; mustard like the fields of sarson in the Punjab; a mellow and gentle lemon yellow; and all the shades of the earth—these were the colours that were woven by the Kancheepuram weaver. The designs for the borders and the pallu cannot be described in words.

The motifs of the temple walls—reflecting the waves and eddies of the rivers and the sea, and the beauty of the serpent represented in the curved line, the circles, squares, and triangles representing the five elements—earth, fire, water, wind, and space—but also reflecting the chakras and the mandalas of ancient philosophies, they wove birds from the forest that were real, as also those from mythology that were imaginative. But most of all, they spun the fabric of their fingers into the yarn and the gentle love of their homes and hearts into the sari, creating six yards and many decades of pure joy!

Conservatism saw the dancer of the early 1900s wear a clumsy pyjama under these gorgeous saris, which made the sari look bulky and untidy. The 1950s saw a carefully pleated and overly tailored 'pyjama costume' replace this, which although more complimentary to the dancer's figure, was not a draped garment by any stretch of imagination, in the way a sari was meant to rise and fall, ebb and flow. Some dancers also wore the 'sari-type' costume which was made to seem as if it was draped, but at a level above the ankles to allow for some movement. But alas, this too did not have the natural flow that a draped garment like the dhoti or the sari enjoys. Every dancer, for the past six decades, has been cutting up this painstakingly made and richly crafted material. It is conceived to suit the dance he or she is performing. What has resulted is every concoction and permutation of 'the drape'. Yet, except for the Manipuri and Odissi and a few male dancers of the South, the costumes for the stage are rarely, if ever, draped. They are stitched.

To hold the fabric, to knot it and drape it, to pleat it and twirl it around the body, and then to feel the fabric fall around one's limbs in a way that enhances the beauty of the fabric and its designs, its border taking on special significance when it holds within itself the araimandi posture and falls gracefully around the ankles when in svastika, is a feeling one cannot adequately describe. It is unadulterated pleasure! And from the point of view of comfort, tailoring stands little chance in comparison. When you watch Bharata Natyam performed on stage, it would seem as though the sari worn by the dancer is, in fact, made for the gods! Deities like Shiva and Vishnu, Kamadev and Sri Krishna, and a host of other mythological characters come to life in the many different dance representations of them on stage. In terms of the fabric, design, and texture of the Kancheepuram silk used, they deserve no less.

Some actor–dancers have the sensitivity to know what colours serve to enhance their personality and the strength of their dance form, and how another tone of colour can highlight an expression of love, or despair. The right colour, the balance between how ornate the zari is, the width of the border, and the length of the pallu can make or ruin a performance. The temple precincts were grand enough to carry the weight of these considerations. But halls differ in size and in weight of performance. It is also true that the personality of the dancer, her age, and comfort level with the garment, matter in how it will look on stage and be appreciated, especially under today's heavy lights.

Textiles, the world over, are markers of the creative genius of a people. To preserve them is to love them for what they are, to enjoy them and wear them, to celebrate their existence in our lives. The dancer has the added opportunity to showcase the garment as a symbol of a culture.

To quote the American painter Robert Henri, 'Art, when really understood, is the province of every human being.' It is also perhaps true that every dance is born, it would seem, of the personality of the dancer and gives back to the personality. It brings form, integration, and enrichment. Creativity is born of a certain personal acumen, in local conditions, woven into a very particular and traditional culture. An appreciation of art can be universal; but art creation is indigenous—so basic is it to who we are.

5

BHARATA NATYAM IN THE
TWENTY-FIRST CENTURY AND
BEYOND

*W*hether it is dance or music or any other pursuit, is it not primarily about one's sensibility, sensitivity, and education—what in India we call our sanskara?

George Arundale, a theosophist and disciple of Annie Besant, said: 'We educate the mind, after a fashion, at the expense of the physical body, which is bad enough, but far worse is our almost total neglect of the feelings, desires, the emotions—of infinitely greater importance these than the mind, though equal in importance to the physical body. We acknowledge the science of mathematics, of chemistry, of physics, of geology, of astronomy. We acknowledge the sciences of geography, of literature, of history, of music, of painting, of craftsmanship. But in the comparatively unevolved state of education there is no place for the science of emotions so rightly stressed in ancient Indian education. This science is a field in itself, and all we have to show for it is a psychology which avoids all that is of vital importance in the constitution of the individual life we are supposed to be educating.'

The fact that our education and now, alas, our arts are for performance, for competition, the fact that they exalt the mind at the expense of all other states of consciousness, stimulating pride in superiority, leads to a grinding demand for unrighteous pre-eminence by the performer, the competitor. These cravings represent a lower aspect of human feeling as compared to one's aspirations, that represent a higher aspect. What may be called the 'body of emotions' is at the core of our being, upon which the intellectual mind and the physical body depend.

Our education in general, and in the arts especially, is essentially about courage and enthusiasm—courage to face life's difficulties, troubles, and frustrations serenely, strongly, cheerfully. And an enthusiasm for the truth, reverence for knowledge systems, understanding the other, compassion and appreciation.

The arts have advanced these values by tapping into our aesthetic and imaginative capacities. As we adapt this objective to the Indian context, a number of philosophical, political, and practical questions come into play, ranging from those of equity of access to arts education for the underprivileged, to ways in which arts education can shape the cultural imagery of a just and equitable society. What are the ways in which the language of art can enable the voicing of alternate experiences, aspirations, and identities that lie outside socially accepted norms?

The value of art for all children cannot be underestimated. Art reflects an interest in the varied expressions of life and nature. The varied expressions of nature, the feelings of people, the nature of discord, and the love for the universe; but also, the unnatural in nature, the inexplicable, that which cannot be understood, that which requires contemplation and reflection—this is the preoccupation of art. You cannot separate art from life, the micro from the macro.

From the very start, in all Indian dance forms, especially the classical, seemingly micro-positions of the fingers called hasta mudras co-ordinate with positions of the head, accompanied by neck and eye movements—which together like a symphony aid and abet the macro movements of the body as a whole. These are considered 'graces' without which the whole has no meaning, almost. It is what happens between two beats that is the magic of dance.

It is akin to placing an object in a room. Where you choose to place it, what angle you place it in, what lies next to it, and what the background to the object is—all these matter. On the other hand, it is arguable that the object can be placed anywhere and it will find its own space.

It is the privilege of the dancer in India to gradually grow into a consciousness of these and of the many other arts and intellectual processes that inform the dance. It never fails to amaze, how varied these other arts are and how their particular fragrance enhances the art of dance. So much so, that without their presence the dance is simply incomplete. These arts were meant to be expressed together, as a single and whole offering. This does not take away from their individual merit or distinction to stand on their own.

You cannot be a sound Bharata Natyam dancer,

for instance, if Indian philosophy, customs, or ritual practices evade you. Certainly, your knowledge of Indian mythology has to be thorough, if not an obsession. India's temple architecture, sculpture, iconography; textiles, and jewellery; its languages, especially the ancient ones like Tamizh, Sanskrit, and Telugu—their prose, poetry, and recitation, vocal and instrumental music—the language of rhythm; a knowledge of the six seasons in nature and the their unmistakable connect to our five senses, physiology, anatomy, yogic practice, reeti-rivaaz or customary practice both past and present; as also sampradaya or propriety—where every nation or society has a different notion of these. The list of these interdependent knowledge systems is truly endless for a dancer. But most important, and perhaps least talked about, is philosophy.

You only have to look at our myths and Puranas to know how complicated our concept of the truth is, as also the lush fertility of our imagination! In the epics of India, at first glance incidents seem like yesterday, today, and tomorrow. Actually, in time–space it could be a lifetime, an avatar or a yuga even, that separates these incidents. This is 'us'. We do not conform to linear time. Our lives are punctuated by events that are cyclical in nature. In relation to the infinite cycle of time and the mythological concept of time, human existence pales into insignificance. An adept dancer with a sound knowledge of the Puranas, for instance, as seen in senior Kathakali dancers, may well be arguing with his enemy on stage, but relates to the audience a similar incident in the past when the gods and demons fought over a similar matter. This can be boastful in nature, or hilarious even in that he puts paid to the remarks of his illustrious opponent. Moving between mythological space and the present is totally natural for him and the audience gets it.

This, of course, is an actor–dancer's delight! Such an amazing wealth of narrative and audiences who understand them too! In such a scenario, what does the actor who presumably reflects or comments upon this complex society do? In theatre, they do the story as it is written, or do a 'take' on it—which is either hilarious, or pathetic, or blasphemous, or bold, or different. In music, they feed the story nostalgia and have a raga tell it like no narrator can. They give it rise and fall, pathos and bhakti or devotion. In films, they throw in songs that enhance the mood of the moment, they have a comedian funny it up, a villain pepper it up, a gangster blaze it up, a moll sugar it up and, of course, the most 'beauteous' belle of them all—kick-start the whole thing up! I love all these forms of art. But I believe the ploy used in the classical dance forms of this country to be the most unique. In the classical solo traditions, it is nayika, the woman who tells her story. She is a metaphor for male, female, and others. She is the jiva atma, the human soul.

Words that make up stories or poems change for each person according their own experiences, by their particular understanding of language and by the meaning they give those words, by the connotation they have for you at any given time. Those words that once had meaning, however, seem to lose their worth as we move through the passage of life. Many experienced artists use a text to suit an occasion or their mood. The rasika, or viewer, receives this as they see fit. Some do not receive the meaning at all; some receive a meaning that neither the poet nor the dancer intended. Some text also has the capacity to move the rasika without any prior knowledge of its meaning, simply by the power of expression, the power of recitation. It also receives strength from the power of expression invested in it by the particular raga and the voice and rendition of the singer. Artists of exceptional talent like Balasaraswati were able to create 'an experience' for the audience. Then words had little meaning.

The idea, of course, is to transcend meaning. It is necessary to get over the words and transfer them, to look at the soul within words, not be bound by them. They must become the truth for each of us, in our own time.

So where does this leave those amongst us who express themselves differently? Those that do not wish to refer to Hindu mythology and its numerous characters, who wish to make their own stories real. Many of us imagine we are 'thinking dancers' who broke from the norm. In fact, in every generation of folk or classical dancers, of ritualistic or martial art practitioners, from urban or rural landscapes, from lower or higher castes—there were always those who moved the river through new paths. They did not depend upon smoother language skills or fancy degrees. There were movers and shakers in every aspect of the dance and its accompaniment. Even the fingering on the mridangam for a Bharata Natyam recital changed drastically in the 1960s when a young Karaikudi R. Krishnamurthy created empathetic drum patterns for the jaatis of Bharata Natyam that had not been heard before. This is but a tiny example, not the extent of change that was brought about over time. Change came in context, content, and core practice. It came in the text, in the music, and in the form. It happened in what was apparent, as also in the hidden aspects of performance—thought processes. It came about in modern interpretations of traditional texts, as also in traditional expressions of modern texts. Languages were included, process was given due consideration, and myths about the dance exploded.

Those among us who sit on the high horse of

intellectual debate, trying to twist and turn and arrive upon a history that justifies who we are today, are perhaps wasting precious time, missing the forest for the trees. What each of us do should suffice, surely? We each arrive upon the norms we favour according to our propensity and circumstance. This, too, changes due to our 'outer' training and 'inner' conviction, along the journey.

The body remains an enigma, a challenge to every dancer, especially considering the time it takes for a dance art to sit comfortably on you, so that after years, the chosen style feels like a well-worn, cannot-do-without garment, second only to your own nature, becoming a reflection of who you are. What has to be resolved without conflict is the chasm that exists between what we do on stage and who we are. We go beyond the theatre actor in our enactment. We set the stage for our poem by depicting the context of the narrative—nature's mood, its particular situation. Then we assume the role of man or God according to the verse chosen. The dancer may choose to speak to the audience directly, to a parrot, or even address the clouds as she would a close friend. None of these are real. Do they belong to this or that time? Are they representations of people we know or imagine? It is all make-believe, and very plausible for these are metaphors to express our innermost desires. These metaphors allow us to camouflage our own identity so we can be more expressive in a make-believe character other than ourselves. But the longing is of oneself and so, too, the search for the truth of life, the truth of performance.

Some years ago, I was invited to a seminar. I was asked to read a paper, but I danced as well—a kind of 'food for thought' presentation, if you like. A lec-dem, except I was not explaining the dance, but simply talking about my journey with the compositions I was presenting and what concerned me about the dance along that journey. As an introduction, a young dancer said, 'Leela is an example of a classical dancer, unlike me, for instance, who is a "traditional" dancer!' I was taken aback and wondered what he meant. That being traditional meant he lacked classicism? And that I paid no heed to tradition? Dance whichever way you like,

I say, and show the world why you call what you do 'Bharata Natyam'. There is an audience for everyone, sensibilities are shared at every level. Each to his own—live and let live. What survives and is tested by time, is true even if there is no audience for it.

Categories are the bane of our existence! They lack a generosity of spirit. They are technical terms that have little to do with people. I do not wish to be called a 'classical' dancer, if that title turns people away, if the very purpose of the dance is defeated, if it suggests an exclusivity that is not me, and if it is not of the people. The words 'classical' and 'contemporary' are valid English terms, imported from a Western, Eurocentric viewpoint. It suggests a linear history. We believe in the perennial. Do the classical, renaissance, modern, or postmodern periods of different nations suggest the same thing? Even within the context of India, does the classical Gupta period, for instance, coincide with the classical period of an art form like Bharata Natyam? Is it appropriate to use a Western term for an art movement in India or China or Africa without injury to the sense and sensibility of the location and practitioners of that form?

To put the journey into context, I use an illuminating Rig Vedic mantra that speaks of two birds living in the same tree. One is the bhokta, who partakes, who tastes and enjoys the fruits of the tree. The other bird is the drashta, who simply watches, contemplates. The bhokta is seen in paintings and in literature, caught in the web of life, in the varying gait of its joys and sorrows. We are caught up with life, but at the same time a part of us seems to stand aside, watching as our lives mingle with the larger ocean of existence. The drashta, or the one who sees, symbolizes the pilgrim soul in each of us.

The dancer is often seen as the bhokta, enmeshed in life, longing for completeness, yearning for something beyond the parameters of the self. I ask myself whether this is so because her art is visually set in the physical realm. During a performance, the audience, and perhaps the dancer too, is compelled to ask, 'Who is the dancer? What is the dance? Can the two be separated?'

On one level, the physical beauty of the dance and

the dancer, her technical virtuosity, the grace of her gestures, and the brilliance of her apparel enrapture the viewer. But dance is also emotional, for what is life or art without feelings, and the expression of those feelings? It is a reflection not only of life, but of the culture and aesthetic of a nation, expressed through literature, song, architecture, design, colour, and rhythm, as also through a strong sense of individualism. The connection between the individual ego and these elements in nature outside of the self, that are beyond rational assessment—that require perhaps an element of contemplation—has been a challenge to every artist through millennia. I believe that the arts are, at one level, purely personal where the ego of the artist is present—as in a painting or in a performance. And yet, art has a function in the social sphere and must reflect that at some level.

But the ultimate search for the truth of the journey is not unlike the journey of the soul as it attempts to move from the gross to the subtle, from the sensual to the spirit. According to cultural thinker Kapila Vatsyayan, 'The aesthetics of Indian dance evolves from a world view which regards the cosmic process as a dance of the microcosm and the macrocosm, a rhythmic interplay of eternity and flux in an unending movement of involution, evolution and devolution. Man on earth is one amongst all living matter, is integral to nature. He is in ceaseless dialogue with it. All matter is made up of the five elements of water, earth, fire, air and space. The life of man, like the tree and animal, sprouts from the seed or womb, is manifested in diverse ways, flowers and fruits, withers and throws up seeds. The cycle continues unending without beginning and end. Man's distinctiveness lies in his capacity of self-reflection and introspection and the potentiality of conscious awareness that the microcosm of his being—body, mind and consciousness is a symbol of the same processes of the macrocosm. The concept of cyclical time and notions of a still centre which flowers as petals of a lotus or a hub with spokes of a wheel, each denoting the capacity of the expansion of the consciousness in a series of concentric circles, all held together within the periphery of a large circumference are fundamental to a world view.

The dancers concern then, in philosophical terms is not so much with the self or the human body as such, but with the use of the body as an instrument in a manner that the universal might be suggested.'

Can a dancer afford not to know this, either through instinct or acquisition of knowledge? Can we discuss the body without the worldview or the philosophy intrinsic to the art? Much like the seed of an idea that grows in one's mind or the idea of a choreography that is dormant in one's mind, the theory of aesthetics points to all life beginning from the formless, arupa; becoming manifest in multiple forms, rupa; and returning to beyond form, pararupa. This reflects the early introspection, leading to the manifestation of an idea or expression, that then creates dhwani or resonance.

From the time of Gandhi, Tagore, Aurobindo, Vallathol, Vishnu Digambar Paluskar, Kamaladevi Chattopadhyay, and Rukmini Devi, each in his or her own way had suggested that the systems of education adopted in India deprioritized the extant indigenous systems of education—like the tols, pathshalas, gurukulams, madrasas, and monasteries, as also the variety of systems of transmitting knowledge, skills, and technique.

Commenting upon this Vatsyayan said, 'Despite the stature of our leaders, the sensitivity and magnificence of their visions, and the tireless efforts put in by them, there is a lack of coherence at the policy level, which resulted in cultural heritage and crafts remaining outside the pale of institutions of higher learning. The creation of a fine balance is the unfinished agenda. To integrate the rich and diverse living traditions of our cultural heritage with formal systems of education is still a dream for many of us. These stalwarts believed that unless there was equity between the creativity of the hand, the intellectual critical discriminating mind and a pulsating heart, a total human being would not be possible.' Decontextualization and relocation of the arts and crafts of India leads to a new showcasing at the urban level. This derecognizes the basic reality, that our arts were formed and took sustenance from the earth and the elements, which is clearly seeded in the rural context.

Why has this dance form—call it by any name or no name, Bharata Natyam if it pleases you—endured over centuries? My guess is that it is inclusive. It is whole—not unlike the brahman—so that when one or another dancer avoid an aspect of it, it still seems whole. If they choose to alter its form, include other forms into it, it still seems to be able to hold its ground. It absorbs all languages, all musical forms, all manner of abuse, even. It is performed by the elite, by slum children, by the non-believer, and the classicist alike. It lends itself to classical, pop, folk, and bhajanai sampradaya with equal elan. So what is the fuss about, then? When the dance form itself asks for no name or classification, why do we need to know which caste we belong to?